31 Days to a More Peaceful You

Lisa Cline

More Info

Blog:

IAmTrustingGod.com

Books:

The back of this book includes excerpts from each of the books listed below.

<u>This Time</u>

<u>To Know God As Father</u>

<u>31 Days to a More Apologetic You: Why defending Your faith matters</u>

<u>31 Days to a More Joyful You</u>

Lisa Cline

May the LORD give strength to his people!
May the LORD bless his people with peace!
Psalm 29:11, ESV

For every Doctor, every Nurse, and every other person putting their lives on the line to help save the lives of others. You are amazing! Hero is to soft a word!

Lisa Cline

CONTEXT

This book was written during the coronavirus pandemic. Sensing a nudge from God, I wrote the devotional with the view of restoring the peace to some of you who may have lost it. May you sense God's love and concern for you throughout the book. And may the peace of God lead you once again.

Lisa Cline

DAY 1 ~ PEACE FROM GOD

---

*God cannot give us a happiness and
peace apart from Himself, because it is not
there. There is no such thing.*
C. S. Lewis.

When I first thought of writing this book, I thought
that maybe I would write two versions. One for Christians
and one for non-Christians

I supposed that the non-Christian version could
include some uplifting quotes to try to help people attain
peace. But I soon realized that because true peace comes
only from God, it would be hard for me to talk
authentically about peace without including the author of it.

This is because "peace denotes the wholeness,
soundness, and well-being that characterizes God and that
God created in the world." So if we want to see peace, real
peace invade our daily lives and change us from the inside

out, we must give God charge over our lives.

i

Ask Yourself

Have I given my life to God? If not, what is stopping me?

DAY 2 ~ PEACE WITHIN

Peace I leave with you;
my peace I give to you.
Not as the world gives do I give to you.
Let not your hearts be troubled,
neither let them be afraid.
John 14:27, ESV

I believe right now other than knowing our families are well, having enough money to pay the bills, and enough toilet paper (just kidding…kind of) Americans are craving peace, because, let's face it, the world is this crazy place right now. And none of us are sure just how fast we will be able to bounce back when this pandemic is over. But we do not have to spend our days living in the turmoil of uncertainty.

As Christians, we know that we have peace because Jesus said so. And it is not just any peace. The peace that Jesus left is "the peace that comes through knowing that your sins are forgiven, and your guilt is removed. It's the peace you have when the ruler of the universe is reigning in your heart; when you know you have that place in heaven prepared by God's grace."[ii]

We have been given peace; we own it. So though "we may be engulfed in physical or mental strife, there can be peace of soul that rises above all the din and conflict of the world. Despite everything, a Christian can know peace."[iii] And usually, a change of mindset is all that is required to experience it.

Ask yourself

Have I been searching high and low for something to give me peace when Jesus already has?

DAY 3 ~ PERFECT PEACE

You keep him in perfect peace
whose mind is stayed on you,
because he trusts in you.
Isaiah 26:3, ESV

It's interesting to note that "the Hebrew expression translated *perfect peace* is literally 'peace, peace.'"[iv] This translation makes sense because it is possible to have an uneasy peace about something, which means we're kind of trusting that things will go well but are not quite sure that they will. Thus to have a *peaceful peace* is to be untroubled by any despairing thoughts.

The word for peace is *Shalom*. Isaiah was using it in terms of a cessation of war. But it means much more than that. Shalom also "includes blessings such as wholeness, health, the quietness of soul, preservation, and completeness."[v].

There may be some who are reading this who need rest from their thoughts. Who have spent years going over and over and over things in their minds, trying to figure "it" all out. Some, while they know that Jesus left them peace, don't seem to understand how to apply it to their lives.

This verse gives them, and us all the solution. We are to turn to God completely, focus on Him and what He is leading us to do, instead of our problems, and he will keep us in that perfect peace that we so desire.

Ask yourself

Have I been worrying about my problems or trusting God?

DAY 4 ~ PEACE THROUGH

PRAYER

Do not be anxious about anything, but
in everything by prayer and supplication with
thanksgiving, let your requests be made known
to God. And the peace of God, which surpasses
all understanding, will guard your hearts and
your minds in Christ Jesus.
Philippians 4:6–7, ESV

As Christians, we need to be so sensitive of whether we are in peace or not that we can quickly tell when we are out of it. So that we may turn to God in prayer. As we release our fears to God, He will rise that peace within us and cover us with it. Granted, it isn't always easy to remember to check our feelings when we are feeling anxious, but as we start to make it a habit, it will get easier. In the past, I had put up notes on the wall to remind myself,

I don't need them anymore, but they did the trick at the time.

How easy it is for the enemy to shut us down by causing us to worry. We must not allow him to do this anymore. When soldiers get attacked, they do what their commander has trained them to do. When we get bombarded with worry, we must do what God has called us to do. Go to him *in everything by prayer and supplication with thanksgiving, let your requests be made known to God.* If we learn to turn to God during these times of trials, He will ease our fears so that we may truly live in our peace. It is then that the world will be transformed as God does a mighty work in and through us.

God is trustworthy; He loves you, and He has a plan for your life that He wants to show you as you connect with him through prayer.

Lisa Cline

Ask yourself

Do I feel like I can trust God with my fears? Am I willing to go to him in prayer, pouring out all my fears and worries, Believing that He will come through for me?

DAY 5 ~ PEACE WALK

The Christian needs to walk in peace,
so no matter what happens, they will be able to
bear witness to a watching world.
Henry Blackaby

There is a reason that God didn't take us home to be with him the moment that we became Christians. And surprisingly, it doesn't really have anything to do with us. It has to do with all the other people that we may reach by our staying. How else could non-Christians be witnessed to if not for us?

When I first became a Christian, there were a lot of people I knew who were on the fence about Christianity. If faith came up in a conversation, they were willing to hear me out.

Now those same people will not listen. They say that Christians have shown by their actions that they only care about themselves and having the world precisely the way they want it. `We don't need to tear down other people to get what we want. We need to trust God to give us what we need and walk in peace as a result of that trust.

Even if we don't realize it, people are watching us. And the reality is that they are judging our faith through our actions. It may not be fair, but that is the truth of it.

It's not a choice whether or not we want to walk out this peace that Jesus gave us. It's something that we need to be doing daily, so that we may show a hurting world the love of Christ.

Ask yourself

What do my actions speak about my faith?

DAY 6 ~ PEACEFUL DWELLING

My people will abide in a peaceful habitation, in secure dwellings, and in quiet resting places.
Isaiah 32:18, (ESV)

As I write this, we (the world) are living in a time as I have never witnessed. It is a scary time for many people as they are mandated to stay in their homes, have been laid off, or have lost their jobs with no future income insight. I know of four people that share an apartment. Out of four of them, three have been laid-off directly because of the virus, and their corporate landlord said that they are not going to adjust or put off the rent.

Looking at the circumstances, we find ourselves in may cause us to feel as if our future is very uncertain, but as Christians, we do not look by eyes of sight, but faith, knowing that we are not alone. God sees what is happening in our lives and will not leave without hope.

I have a friend who, about five or six years ago, was in a position where she was going to lose her beautiful home due to finances. One day she was supposed to sign some papers for a short sale, but God got me up early and gave me a word for her. I felt that she was not supposed to sign but hold on, trusting him. A phrase I used in conveying the message confirmed what God had already spoken to her. Long story short, even though her future in that house looked bleak at that point, she is still in her home today. God made away. She didn't lose it.

Isaiah wrote the verse above to a people who lived in a land where just about anything went. This made some fearful, "however, God promised to intervene. The city would be secure, not because of its walls, but because the Spirit would defend it."[vi]

Take heart, dear people, you are not alone in what

you're going through. The Spirit of the Lord who defended the Israelites is still alive and will protect and keep you today.

Ask Yourself

God has promised me that I *will abide in a peaceful habitation*. Do I believe it?

DAY 7 ~ PEACEFUL

RELATIONSHIPS

We are not at peace with others
because we are not at peace with
ourselves,
and we are not at peace with ourselves
because we are not at peace with God
Thomas Merton

In my early 30s, I was a stressed-out miserable, angry, unhappy person. I felt the world had done me wrong. I was perpetually mad and didn't feel good about myself. And thoughts of abandoning this life often came to my mind.

That all changed when I made the decision to trust God and follow His lead. Immediately, He started to show me that I had to make peace with myself and who I was. To love who he created me to be. And then I had to make peace with others and love them and see them as who He created them to be.

One of the first things God changed in me was my desire to hold a grudge. I remember how one second God led me to surrendered my right to hold a grudge against others, and the next second there was a knock at the door by someone that I held a grudge against. It was one of my neighbors who had treated me badly (I felt). God wanted *me* to apologize and make it right with *them* (can you believe it). I absolutely did not want to apologize to *them*. *They* were the problem, not *me,* I felt. God adjusted that attitude real quick, and in the end, I knew that He wasn't going to change his mind, and I wasn't going to ignore him, so I did what he asked and apologized. Immediately upon apologizing, I felt refreshed and revived. I realized that I had been at fault as well as the neighbor. Later that day, the only other person I had an active grudge against was put in my path. I ended up making peace with them, as well.

I realized that I was wasting so much of my time just thinking about how they had wronged me that I was not living my life—actively seeking the best that it has to offer.

Life is too short to waste it on grudges. Do what you have to do to live a peaceful life. Make sure your relationship with God is authentic. When it comes to conflicts with yourself or with other people, bring them directly to God and ask Him to help you heal your pain, restore your peace, and move on.

Ask Yourself

Am I at peace with God?

Am I at peace with myself?

Am I at peace with others?

DAY 8 ~ PEACEFUL WORLD

"Peace comes from being able to contribute the best that we have, and all that we are, toward creating a world that supports everyone. But it is also securing the space for others to contribute the best that they have and all that they are."
Hafsat Abiola

If we want to live a life of peace, we must make peace with the fact that other people in this world don't live the way we may want them to.

It is not our job to police the world. It is our job to be the hands and feet of our Savior.

Nobody ever forced me to be who I am today. I became who I am through a process led by God, who gave me the freedom and the guidance that I needed to explore and make choices that I felt were right for me.

Everybody must have that right to come to God

freely. God is the one who changes hearts, and God is the one who convicts.

Pray for those you love and pray for those you don't. Ask God to help you be more loving and Pray for the salvation of others. All that is good.

But please do not try and shame anyone into coming to God. All you will do is keep them from what they assume is a hateful God. And you will most likely, lose your peace in the process.

Ask yourself

What people in my community can I extend grace to?

DAY 9 ~ SEWING PEACE

If we have no peace, it is
because we have
forgotten that we belong
to each other."
Mother Teresa

The coronavirus has not just devastated families. It has done damage to an already fractured America. Political parties are fighting against each other. People are attacking Asian Americans with fists and knives (as in the case of a six-year-old child and his family). Food is getting hard to find for lower-income people, and nerves are frayed. It is clear to see that peace is needed more now than ever.

That said, I understand how frustrating it can be when you want to be heard, and though you believe you are talking English, the other side responds as if you were speaking an alien language. It is easy to get mad. But that is not how God calls us to act.:

"Be angry and do not sin; ...and give no opportunity to the devil. ... Let no corrupting talk come out of your mouths, but only such as is good for building up, as fits the occasion, that it may give grace to those who hear. And do not grieve the Holy Spirit of God, by whom you were sealed for the day of redemption. Let all bitterness and wrath and anger and clamor and slander be put away from you, along with all malice."
(Ephesians 4:26, 27 29-31, ESV)

Anger never won over anybody. Neither did name-calling. If we are stooping to that level, that means we have not done enough research to prove our point. If we're going to make a difference, we must be able to debate another person respectfully and peacefully.

I used to listen to Dr. Walter Martin's (an apologetic) teachings often. Before a teaching on a cult, he would remind people that he wasn't there because he hated the cult members but because he loved them and wanted them to know the truth about Jesus. Who he disliked was the organization that was keeping its members from knowing the truth about God.

There are always going to be people that believe

differently than us. We must love the person and be respectful of them as God calls us to be, regardless of their beliefs.

Desmond Tutu once said, "Don't raise your voice, improve your argument."

Let us sew peace through improving our way of debating with others.

Ask yourself

How am I sewing peace

DAY 10 ~ PEACEFUL START

A great many people are trying
to make peace,
but that has already been done.
God has not left it for us to do;
all we have to do is to enter into it.
Dwight L. Moody

Just a reminder That Jesus has left us with peace. We have it, but how do we enter into it? Isaiah 57:2 tells us that *Those who walk uprightly enter into peace* (NIV).

To walk uprightly is to do "that which is just and proper."[vii] Interestingly, just one verse earlier is about how "an observer notes the collapse of order and justice in the city."[viii] So this peace is a promise that "anticipates not merely a cessation of hostilities but also the return of a healthy social order and a just application of law."[ix] And if we ever needed that in our country it would be now.

As of today (4/1/2020), we are told that as many as

Lisa Cline

240,000 more people may die before this is all over. That is

a horrific number, but we do not have to panic. Jesus has

left us with peace.

If we are ever to be a people who shine our light so

bright that others may see the truth of who God is, if we're

ever to be people who would show the world that we are

Christians by acts of love that we sacrificially give, it

would be now.

May we all take time in the morning to dedicate our

day to God, asking Him to lead us in peace, so that we may

comfort others with it.

Ask yourself

How do I start my day? What do I need to change?

DAY 11 ~ SMILING

PEACEFULLY

Peace Begins with a smile
Mother Teresa

Everyone's favorite Christmas movie at our house is the movie *Elf*. "I like smiling. Smiling's my favorite," is probably our favorite line from it. I mean, how can you not help but smile when you hear that line!

And there is a reason that smiling should be everyone's favorite. "Smiling activates the release of feel-good-messengers that work towards fighting stress …[That] dopamine, endorphins [natural pain killers] and serotonin are all released into your bloodstream, making not only your body relax but also work to lower your heart rate and blood pressure."[x] It's pretty amazing isn't it that God created us in such a way that by choosing to smile, we get the physical and mental lift that we need.

So if you find yourself stressed out, it may help you too smile a few times and kickstart the system that God put in place to help you find the peace within.

Ask yourself

Have I smiled today?

DAY 12 ~ SLEEPING PEACEFULLY

In peace, I will lie down

and sleep,

for you alone, Lord,

make me dwell in safety.

Psalm 4:8

When David the King wrote this Psalm, some believe he was in the midst of what was called *Absalom's Rebellion*. That was a time when King David's son Absalom tried to take the throne away from Him. So he, out of fear for his life, was on the run and most likely was in danger of being killed. Again, by his own child (talk about a difficult child).

That David had a little bit of pressure on him was very much an understatement. But, look again at what he says during that time. *In peace, I will lie down and sleep for you alone Lord make me dwell in safety.* Even though he had every reason to be terrified and anxious and have all kinds of trouble sleeping, he didn't because he knew that God was with him. Steven J. Lawson "writes of this psalm: 'Life should be lived with the assurance of God's sovereignty, knowing that He rules over everything for his glory. Even when it seems as if the ungodly have dominated the scene, believers should remember that God has chosen the godly for himself and will not forsake them. This is the central message of Psalm 4, a song that provides a Godward focus in the midst of life's storms."[xi] When your boat is rocking, and you feel it may go under, remember that *God has chosen the godly for himself and will not forsake them.*

Today we're dealing with the ungodly virus that has dominated the world scene. Tomorrow it may be another virus, or a war, or maybe a lost job, or a sick child, or something else that has rocked our world, But remember that you're a child of God He will not forsake you. He is with you in the middle of your storms. Turn to him, and he will be there, helping you to sleep peacefully once again.

Ask yourself

Are you soaking in God's peace

DAY 13 ~ PEACEFUL FILLING

As we pour out our bitterness,
God pours in his peace.
F.B. Meyer

At first glance, one might read that quote and say, "I'm not bitter. That's not who I am. I don't have any bitterness in me, so this must not apply." But looking at the Eerdmans Bible Dictionary, which defines bitterness as "something disagreeable to the sense of taste,"[xii] might just change your mind.

Haven't we all had situations or dealings with people who have left a disagreeable taste in our mouths? It's easy to get a little bitter about a lot of things and to have that bitterness just sit there and fester until before we realize it, we are filled with so much bitterness that there is just no way that we can walk in the peace and freedom that Christ died to give us.

I encourage you to prayerfully ask God what things you might be holding inside that you're bitter about. Write them down if you need to. Then ask Him to help you to let it go, and fill you with peace.

Ask yourself

What things give me a bad taste in my mouth?

DAY 14~ PEACE CALLING

The mind governed by the flesh is death,

but the mind governed by the Spirit

is life and peace.

Romans 8:6

The Greek word for *mind* translates "phronema, which can be rendered "mind-set"; It is the "faculty of fixing one's mind on some way of thinking… focus on strong intention aim, aspiration, striving"[xiii] So what Paul is saying here is, "The lifestyle of the flesh flows from a mind oriented to the flesh, whereas the lifestyle of the Spirit comes from a mind oriented to the Spirit."[xiv] It "denotes the basic direction of a person's will."[xv]

If we want to live a life full of peace, we must keep our minds focused on the things of God and our ears tuned to hear his voice. This is "because God speaks in "a still, small voice" (1 Kings 19:12), which may partially explain why we find it hard to hear him when he speaks. It's much like receiving a phone call in a house with the T.V. going, the stereo blaring, and a house full of people chatting with one another. To understand the caller, it requires asking the friends to be quiet and turn down the stereo and T.V.So it is with hearing God. It may well require removing those distractions, those areas of sin that deafen our ears to the voice of the Lord."[xvi]

As we become more familiar with hearing God's voice, it will be easier to tell when he is speaking

Ask yourself

What orientation is my mindset?

DAY 15 ~ RIGHTEOUS PEACE

Therefore, since we have been justified
by faith, we have peace with God through our
Lord Jesus Christ.
Romans 5:1, ESV

Often we don't have peace because we don't feel like God has really forgiven us for our sins. Sins are generally something that one does not want to talk about openly. Because of this, it is easy to feel like you are the only one that still messes up. This can make one feel like they do not really belong as part of that church family or that group of Christian friends.

Look again at Romans 5:1. We are justified through our faith in Jesus. To be justified means "to be shown or declared to be righteous or in the right."[xvii] To take it a step further, we see that The act of declaring someone righteous means to "acquit, to set free, to remove guilt, acquittal.'…

'from all (the sins)."[xviii] I love what it says of this in Louw-Nida, "in a number of languages the process of acquittal takes the form of a direct statement, for example, 'to say, You are not guilty' or '…, You no longer have sin' or, as expressed idiomatically in some instances, '…, Sin is no longer on your head'."[xix]

How wonderful is that? The weight of your sins is no longer upon your head. How freeing is it to know that if you have placed your faith in Jesus, no devil in hell can say a thing against you because you have been shown to be in the right.

The weight of your sins has been removed. You are free to live your life in peace, knowing that

If you haven't given your life to Jesus see Salvation Prayer

Ask yourself

Do I feel that I have been justified by faith?

DAY 16 ~ PEACEFUL DECISIONS

True peace consists in not separating ourselves from the will of God.
Thomas Aquinas

Prayer is an integral part of the Christian faith. Still, we don't have to pray about every decision we're going to make. Which is a good thing because it is estimated "that an adult makes about 35,000 conscious decisions each day."[xx] I don't know about you, but I don't have that kind of time on my hands.

Instead of praying over every decision, we just need to pray to God and ask Him to keep us in His perfect will. Then when we're going through our day, and we start to lose our peace about doing a particular thing, we can make a choice to steer clear of it or pray about it.

Sometimes when I have a massive decision before me and trusting my peace doesn't feel substantial enough, I will just go to God and say. I believe I should do [name thing]. I am going to go in pursuit of it. If you do not want me to, then please shut the door. Every single time I have prayed that prayer, God has been faithful in closing doors that needed to be closed and opening doors that needed to be opened. He hears our prayers. We can walk in peace as we follow Him.

Ask yourself

Do I let peace guide me?

DAY 17 ~ PEACEFUL THANKS

Being thankful can reap
many benefits for you,
like peace and joy.
Jeff & Michelle Niederstadt

A few times in my life, when I was younger, I have had significant bouts of depression. That aside, I see that the periods where I was the most upset and the angriest were the periods where I was the most unthankful.

There was one period where I saw my kids going through hard things. This caused me to despair and question why God would allow it. *Did He not love my children as much as others?* I wondered. The more I thought about what He had not done for my children (compared to others), the sadder I became until I lost all sense of any peace that I had known.

It was then a friend challenged me. She asked me if

I have been paying as much attention to the things that God had done for my children as the things I believe he hasn't.

Of course, the answer was no. I am not sure what exactly I did from that point on to change my outlook. But I do know that I made a habit of thanking God for the things that He has done.

This, I am sure, brought my peace back, and I am determined never again to be anything less than thankful, for God has been so very good to me.

Start to count your blessings when you find yourself becoming down, be thankful, and God will restore your peace.

Ask yourself

Do I thank God for what He has done for me?

DAY 18 ~ GENTLE PEACE

Peace cannot be achieved through
violence; it can only
be attained through understanding.
Ralph Waldo Emerson

I stopped watching the news long ago, but I know that if I were to turn it on today, I would see a lot of angry, violent people doing a lot of horrible things. Some may be an accident, and some may be planned. But the violence is guaranteed to be shown because that's what sells.

We are in a time like I never thought I would see. Sadly I have seen so many people screaming and yelling about how horrible everybody is. How we need to "take back what is ours." My heart breaks when I see this. Because Christians should not be following this path of anger. Shouting without words, but actions. "It belongs to us, not you" or "Our way is the only way! Comply or get out!"

We demand compliance immediately from people who are dissimilar to us. We don't give anybody that chance to grow as we have.

The thing is I never saw Jesus do that. I never saw him storm the government demanding everyone live precisely as he says. As His disciples, we need to think about who we are following. Who has our ultimate allegiance, God, or country?

> *"Come to me, all who labor and are heavy laden,*
> *and I will give you rest.*
> *Take my yoke upon you, and learn from me,*
> *for I am gentle and lowly in heart,*
> *and you will find rest for your souls.*
> *For my yoke is easy, and my burden is light.""*
> Matthew 11:28–30, (ESV)

Jesus says he is gentle, and I believe him. As his disciples, we should be gentle too. No one was ever won over by anger and shaming. If we want to live a life of peace, then we need to remember to keep our peace, when it comes to others.

55

Ask yourself

Has any anger that I have ever had towards others ever helped me to be peaceful? Am I praying for those I oppose?

DAY 19 ~ CHOOSING PEACE

Making peace with your
own backstory,
and accepting that not all
of it is good, is vital.
Fearne Cotton

Even though you may sometimes feel like you're

the only one that has experienced a difficult childhood, or

you're the only one that has "this problem person" in your

life, or even that you are the unluckiest person that has ever

lived, it is simply not true! The enemy always tries to

shame us into believing that we are the only ones to deal

with something hard. He does this because he knows that if

he can make us feel bad about who we are, then he can

steal our peace. This immobilizes us so that we have a hard

time moving forward.

Your life is not just about what has happened to you

in the past, whether you chose what happened or not. Your

life will be determined by the choices you make going forward as well.

It's not easy, but you have to let your past go if you want to move forward in peace.

It is something that I have had to do, or I would have remained stuck forever, unhappy, and complaining about what "they" did to me.

I still have periods when shame will wash over me. But I know now that I have to run back to God and ask for Him to help me to get my peace back. I have to choose to let go of the past and go forward with God.

If you're feeling shame or anger about your past or if you just feel like you are dying inside, Go to God and talk to Him. Ask him to help you and then go to look in the mirror and tell yourself that you are more than your past. You are a beloved child of God.

Ask yourself

Have I processed with God those past events that are stealing my peace?

DAY 20 ~ PEACEFUL

FOUNDATION

The foundation of the Christian's peace is everlasting; it is what no time, no change can destroy. It will remain when the body dies; it will remain when the mountains depart and the hills shall be removed, and when the heavens shall be rolled together as a scroll. The fountain of His comfort shall never be diminished, and the stream shall never be dried.His comfort and joy is a living spring in the soul, a well of water springing up to everlasting life.
Jonathan Edwards

I've seen some pretty funny videos lately about parents who are stuck in their homes with high maintenance children. It is both hilarious and telling of the level of anxiety many people are feeling right now. But we must remember that although it may feel right now as if things will never get back to normal, they will. Schools will reopen, businesses will keep trading, and you will be able to find yourself once again relaxing in a movie theater in a chair that is sure to put you to sleep if you are past the age of thirty.

But I get that it feels crazy right now, overwhelming even. Bills are piling up, children are at boredom-level-cross-country-road-trip in a car, Yet still, *the foundation of the Christian's peace is everlasting; it is what no time, no change can destroy.*

And I realize how chaotic things can get for some (I have a five-year-old grandson who lives with me), but we have to at some point rise above all the chaos and be determined people of God who are going to live in peace. I honestly believe that this is a time like no other to show others what it means to be a real Christian who walks close with God an allows peace to invade their world. So when your unsaved spouse is rude to you, or your boss is demanding things be done immediately, though you lack the proper resources, You will be able to shine your light, remain calm in your storm, and they will be able to see there's a difference.

Ask Yourself

Do I see today as a time to make a difference through my peacefulness?

DAY 21 ~ PEACEFUL MUSIC

God's peace comes when I
choose to worship instead of worry.
Renee Swope

In all the years that I have been a Christian, I have felt that there is nothing that helps me enter into the peaceful presence of God more than worship music. It is incredible how easily I enter into peace when it is turned on.

And not only does peace enter, but anger and strife flee. Long ago, I was told that if there was a disagreement or there was tension in my house or if the air was so thick with conflict that I couldn't breathe, that I was to turn it on.

When my husband was alive, and we would get into disagreements, I would put worship music on. Immediately the anger was dissipated. When I was a single mom, with some children that were having a hard time dealing with the loss of their father, and things would get hard, I would put worship music on, and peace would flood our house.

I do not believe the enemy can stay in a house where there is worship music.

Yes, with what's happening right now, we should be very concerned. We should take steps doing all we can through social distancing and washing hands to make sure that we're not getting sick or passing it on to a loved one.

But after this virus ends, something else will come up that will try and cause us to worry. There's always going to be something to worry about if we choose to. However, God doesn't cause us to worry; he calls us to trust him.

So remember the next time you're having a hard time, put worship music on and praise God. Or better yet, start your day with praising God and allow that peace to flow out through you throughout the rest of the day to others who are in desperate need of it.

Ask yourself

How often do I listen to worship music? How much do I want a peaceful home?

DAY 22 ~ DOING PEACE

You will find peace not by
trying to escape your problems,
but by confronting them
courageously.
You will find peace not in
denial, but in victory.
J. Donald Walters

Some of us have more problems than others, but we all have issues. Sometimes our problems can pile up because we don't want to deal with them.

I once knew a girl that had a specific problem that she needed to deal with. And she spent six months avoiding it before finally deciding to take care of it. When she did, she was surprised to find that it only took her 1/2 hour, and it was solved. She never had to deal with it again.

How familiar does that story sound? How many of us can say that we have wasted too much of our lives worrying about a problem that didn't end up being a problem in the end?

Now granted, some problems are more significant than others. I get that some of us are facing some pretty rough things, but if you have a problem in your life that God is calling you to confront and you're not doing it because you're afraid, here's your sign. God wants you to deal with it because He knows that you can never be fully at peace until you do.

If you are afraid, ask God for His help. You're not alone. He will make a way through all of it. He will never abandon you!

I have wasted too much time because I thought problems were insurmountable, or worth putting off. I am determined not to lose anymore. Because for every moment lost, is one that could have been spent peacefully living my life for God.

Lisa Cline

Ask yourself

Am I putting off things that God is calling me to take care of today?

DAY 23 ~ PEACEFUL

DEALINGS

Peace is not the
absence of conflict,
it is the ability to handle conflict
by peaceful means.
Ronald Reagan

As Christians, we're to be people of peace. Not just in and of ourselves but in our dealings with others. I was married almost nineteen years to my late husband. If I am honest, the first ten years were a free for all. I wasn't following God at the time, and neither was he. Things would get pretty heated at times. In the next eight years of our marriage, I was walking out my faith. As I grew in it, the conflicts became less and less. I was usually the source of the battles, as he was pretty easygoing. When he became a Christian shortly before his death, the conflicts were almost nonexistent. This isn't because we magically became fairies floating on clouds; it's because we learned how to handle disputes by peaceful means. We started to value **us** more than we valued getting our way. God taught us tools that helped us keep our peace.

This life is full of a lot of difficult people. It just is. And we are bound to run into them from time to time. Sometimes in the store or the apartment laundry room, our kitchen, or even our bathroom mirror. They are everywhere. So solving conflict through peaceful means needs to be our goal. To that end, Stephen Hopson has listed seven ways to do just that. They are:[xxi]

1. Remain calm.

2. Let the other person do the talking until they are talked out.

3. Genuinely consider the other person's point of view.

4. Use words that convey that you are listening.

5. If the situation turns verbally abusive, put a stop to it.

6. If you are wrong, quickly admit it and take responsibility.

7. Use the power of visualization.

I wasted way too much time conflicting with my husband. I wish I could have that time back so that I could just enjoy being with him.

If I could have the chance to do it all again, I would spend more time asking God for help, and then do as he called me to do.

Don't let conflict with others ruin your peace. Learn how to solve conflict and save your peace.

Ask yourself

Am I skilled at resolving conflict, or do I need to learn how to?

DAY 24 ~ EXPENSIVE PEACE

---

*Anything that costs you
your peace is too expensive.*

When I was a young mother, I used to walk to the store with my two young children to get the food we needed. It was a little bit away from my house, and I didn't drive, so it was not something I loved to do.

One day after getting home, I realized that the cashier had given me back too much change. Twenty dollars too much. It was tempting to keep it because back then, twenty dollars was a lot of money, and we were very poor at the time. But though I really could have used it, and even though I was saved but not fully living for God at the time, I knew that God wanted me to take it back.

I had lost all peace over keeping it. So even though I was not thrilled about what I was about to do, I turned around and went back to the store (in the rain no less), handed the money back to the cashier. She asked me why I would give it back when I was already home. Then she hinted that I could just keep it. I just shook my head no and gave it back and immediately was flooded with peace. That twenty was not worth the price of losing my peace.

If you have something that you're contemplating doing that could take away your peace, don't do it!If you have done something that has caused you to lose your peace, ask God what to do to make it right.

Every moment we are given is spent doing something. Make it count.

Ask yourself

Has something caused me to lose my peace that I can do something about?

DAY 25 ~ PEACEFUL

PRESENT

If you are depressed,
you are living in the past
if you are anxious
you are living in the future,
if you are at peace,
you are living in the present.
Lao Tzu

When my husband died eleven years ago, I made some pretty foolish decisions. Now don't get me wrong, I made some pretty good ones too. But some were cringe-worthy. Usually, the bad ones I made had to do with the fact that I wasn't living in the moment. I missed my husband so terribly and tried to fill the void in attempting to make things happen instead of just letting them happen naturally.

I tried to force a relationship to go to the next level. I wanted the link to be immediately the same as I had with my husband. I was grieving and in no state to be with anybody, let alone somebody I thought there was a future with. Really, I just wanted to make the pain go away by making something happen that wasn't there. And I wanted my future to be ok. All of this caused me a lot of anxiety. Anxiety that I didn't need to be dealing with, and at a time where I should have been focused on my family.

Eventually, God allowed me to see what was going on because I gave him enough of my time for him to do so. It's not that he wasn't standing in front of me waving big red flags. I was just choosing to ignore him.

If you've gone through loss, you know that it can be challenging to live in the present. But it's the only way that you'll be able to process your loss and move on to the future that God has for you

What I have since realized is that I don't need a

relationship to make me feel joyful, peaceful, and happy. That I can be in the moment and enjoy my friends, family, writing, and enjoy school. And that I am whole all by myself. I do not need to postpone my peace until another person comes into my life. I have all I need with God.

Ask yourself

Do I live in the present?

DAY 26 ~ TRUSTING PEACE

---

*When a man's ways please
the LORD, He makes even his
enemies to be at peace with him.*
Proverb 16:7

When we are on the right track, doing what God has called us to do, "the enemy," Satan will often throw someone or something across our paths to try and do us harm. When this happens, we do not need to fear. God is in control. That is the key to keeping your peace, even through trying times.

Now God making our enemies at peace with us doesn't necessarily mean that we're going to be best friends (though it has happened), but it does mean that God will work things out for our ultimate good.

We need to keep a check on our fear. While there is healthy fear (fear of burning your hand makes you careful around the burner), there is an unhealthy fear that can stop you in your tracks. Dr. Paul Tournier "observes that "fear creates what it fears. Fear of war compels a country to take the very measures which unleash war. The fear of losing the love of a loved one provokes us to just that lack of frankness, which undermines love. The skier falls as soon as he begins to be afraid of falling. Fear of failing in an examination takes away the candidate's presence of mind and makes success more difficult."[xxii]

The dividing line between the two types of fear is always God. If you are unsure of ignoring something or doing something about it to protect yourself and your family, go to God in prayer (and wise counsel) and trust God by not feeding your fear by thinking about it and talking about it. And then ask yourself how you can best witness to others through your actions and words. Because nothing speaks louder to an unbeliever than a Christian who is going through a hard time but keeps their peace.

Ask yourself

Are you fearful? How you brought it to God?

DAY 27 ~ PRACTICE PEACE

Peace is a daily, a weekly, a monthly
process,
gradually changing opinions, slowly
eroding old barriers,
quietly building new structures.
John F. Kennedy

Just like with anything else in life, if we want to become naturals at keeping our peace, we must work at it.

When I was a young adult, I used to be very anxious over losing anything. It didn't matter what it was, a bank card, a book, a sock, a lego piece, anything missing caused me anxiety. I would get more and more and more anxious as time wore on. My peace flew out of the door once I realized something was gone. Eventually, I would end up tearing up the house, turning over everything. As you can imagine, it wasn't such a great witness to my children, nor was it helpful to me. When I got serious about keeping my peace, I asked God to help me. He immediately showed me where the anxiety was coming from. That it was more about my feeling uncomplete than it was about the item.

In the years since that day, I've seen such a difference in the way that I react when I lose things, even important things, as I allowed my pursuit of peace to trump my feelings (feelings are fickle anyway. Do what is right, and they will follow). Yesterday my son lost his wallet. The old me would have been tearing through the house, looking through everything. He knew this and told me, "Don't worry about it. I will take care of it." I started feeling anxious, but remembering to practice peace, I let it go. He found his wallet the next morning. While the old me would have lost sleep over it, the new me slept like a baby.

I encourage you just to dig in. Keep doing the work. And before you know it, you will appear as if you were born with a peaceful disposition.

Lisa Cline

Ask yourself

What are the areas of my life that I need to practice
my peace in?

DAY 28 ~ PEACEFUL

CONSEQUENCES

Peace brings with it so
many positive emotions
that it is worth aiming for
in all circumstances.
Estella Eliot

I once asked my mom (who was only 40 at the time) if getting older bothered her. She said, "It beats the alternative." One might say the same thing about peace.

Being at peace opens the door for us to experience things like awe, excitement, wonder, contentment, confidence, surprise, cheerfulness, inspiration, hope, gratitude, to name a few.

The opposite is true when we are not. One of the first things I notice when I lose my peace is the loss of creativity. It is nearly impossible for me to focus.

Lisa Cline

Another thing that can be affected is relationships. How many fights were started at home because someone lost their peace at the office?

I once saw an episode of Touched by an Angel where they traced two storylines. One of them showed how lives were affected by a person who (in peace) said a kind word. The other showed the opposite. Though it was fiction, it was a startling depiction of how important it is for us to act towards others with kindness. We never know the load that someone carries.

So not only does our staying in peace help us, but it opens the door to our sowing good seeds in the lives of others.

Ask yourself

Why is it important to me that I keep my peace?

DAY 29 ~ SLOW PEACE

Blessed are the single-
hearted, for they shall enjoy much
peace.. If you refuse to be hurried
and pressed, if you stay your soul
on God, nothing can keep you from
that clearness of spirit which is life
and peace. In that stillness you
know what His will is.
Amy Carmichael

I am a multitasker. I like to have laundry going, dishes drying, and food cooking, while I am talking on the phone and cleaning the livingroom. All that is ok as long as I take my time. But if I try and hurry it up, I almost always lose my peace in the process. I find myself wanting to mutter aloud about how hard I work, and thoughts of "it would be nice if I had a maid like you do" float through my mind toward my family but hopefully not out of my mouth.

Because I am a goal-oriented person, I really enjoy

cleaning, as long as I am not rushed. The problem isn't with doing; it is with my state of mind.

If you find yourself losing your peace, consider slowing down the pace of what you are doing and see if that helps restore you to yourself.

Ask yourself

Can I adjust the things I do so that I no longer have to hurry through them?

DAY 30 ~ POWERFUL PEACE

The day the power of love
overrules the love of power,
the world will know peace.
Mahatma Gandhi

Right after the president said that he was considering opening the country up by Easter (something he ultimately decided against doing) Texas Lt. Governor Dan Patrick ent on tv and insinuated that older Americans should volunteer to die to save the economy. This led to an outpouring of people saying that they do not want "Memaw to die so that they can have nice things." And Bill Gates was quoted as saying that we "Can't reopen business and 'ignore that pile of bodies in the corner.'"

I get that a lot is on the line. America is a rich and powerful country. The policymakers are afraid of losing that. I understand that there is pressure on them, and we are in a tough place right now. But we are a country founded on Christian values. We must not ever think it is ok to trade the lives of people for stuff. There is not one part of the Bible that sanctifies that view.

This book is about walking in peace, and I would be remiss if I did not include a page on the importance of praying for peace within our country.

We need to be people focused on loving others through our actions. Just as we value the life of an unborn baby, we need to value the lives of our older citizens. The day that we trade lives for stuff is the day that we have lost all right to speak about ethics and morality.

We must be praying for our leaders daily. We must be praying for our country daily. We must be praying for the love of Christ to pour out over this country and for the power of love to overrule the love of power.

Ask yourself

Are you praying for your country daily?

DAY 31 ~ GETTING PEACE

---

the LORD lift up his countenance

upon you

and give you peace.

Numbers 6:26 ESV

That is the tail end of a blessing given to Israel. Andrew Knowles writes that this "beautiful blessing is echoed in Psalm 67, where it becomes a prayer that God will bless all the nations through Israel."xxiii We use this blessing today, "for it belongs to us as well as to Israel. This is because the church has been blessed with "every spiritual blessing" through the Lord Jesus Christ (Eph. 1:3), and we can claim this benediction through Him."xxiv

Keep in mind that "with the Law given, the priests ordained, and the sacrificial system which provided for the forgiveness of sin instituted, it was time for God's people to move on…From this point on, Israel would be responsible to God for the choices individuals, groups, and the whole community madexxv1. And because we are responsible for what we have learned, from this point on, we are accountable to God for the choices that we will have made regarding peace. May you cultivate a life rich in peace and filled to the brim with every single good thing that a life lived in peace can bring.

---

[1] Lawrence O. Richards, The Teacher's Commentary (Wheaton, IL: Victor Books, 1987), 124

The LORD bless you and keep you;

the LORD make his face to shine upon you

and be gracious to you;

the LORD lift up his countenance upon you

and give you peace.

(Numbers 6:24–26, ESV)

Ask yourself

Now that I am accountable, what will I do

tomorrow to cultivate this life of peace?

APPENDIX 1 SALVATION

PRAYER

The following is taken **gotquestions.org** If you want to learn more click the link below.

Saying the sinner's prayer is simply a way of declaring to God that you are relying on Jesus Christ as your Savior. There are no "magical" words that result in salvation. It is only faith in Jesus' death and resurrection that can save us. If you understand that you are a sinner and in need of salvation through Jesus Christ, here is a sinner's prayer you can pray to God: "God, I know that I am a sinner. I know that I deserve the consequences of my sin. However, I am trusting in Jesus Christ as my Savior. I believe that His death and resurrection provided for my forgiveness. I trust in Jesus and Jesus alone as my personal

Lisa Cline

Lord and Savior. Thank you Lord, for saving me and

forgiving me! Amen!"[2]

Go to

https://www.gotquestions.org/sinners-prayer.html

For more information

APPENDIX 2 WRITING

EXCERPTS

The following are samplings of each of my currently available books.

To check and see if new books are out please go to my author page

AMAZON

https://www.amazon.com/Lisa-Cline/e/B0079HL1Y6/ref=dp_byline_cont_book_1

GOODREADS

https://www.goodreads.com/author/show/5768875.Lisa_Cline

Lisa Cline

This Time (Fiction)

Prologue

"Who do you think you're talking to?"

"You!" She screamed. "I am talking to you! Do you hear me!"

Natalie looked at the horse, and she knew that she had to time it right.

She formed her plan, knowing that she would have one shot.

She knew that she would be taking a considerable risk. But she had no choice.

To do nothing was no longer an option.

Chapter 1

When Natalie opened her eyes the morning before her 18th anniversary and heard her husband getting ready for work, she smiled.

"Hey, cutie," she called out.

"Hey yourself," He called back.

"You weren't going to run off without giving me a kiss, were you?"

"Have I ever?" He said, poking his head out of the bathroom.

She raised an eyebrow, "Well, there was that one time."

"Ugh. Not that again."

"You know I will never let you live that, down. I mean forgetting to kiss me and forgetting my birthday." She shook her head.

"I was an animal?" He replied.

"Pretty much." She said as he leaned over to kiss her before going to the closet, grabbing a belt and threading it through his pant loops.

"How could you have ever forgotten to kiss these

luscious things?" She said, circling her lips with her finger.

"The world may never know." He sighed as he grabbed his jacket.

"Wait, before you go, can you give me a lift." She said, throwing the covers off.

"Where?"

"Well, Canada sounds nice. But I was thinking to my feet."

Sam took her hand and helped her to her feet and then leaned over and kissed her swollen belly. "Only three more months until you are here. I cannot wait to meet you, my little linebacker."

"Or artist, cook, dancer, singer, or seamstress." She added. "We are not in the dark ages. There is no telling what path he will choose to follow."

"I think the word that you are looking for is a clothier." He said smugly. "Anyway, as long as that path doesn't lead him to the jail or the morgue, I will be happy."

She looked at Sam. Oh, how she loved him, loved their way of bantering. "You know I would have got that word right if I didn't have this mom-brain."

"Mom-brain?"

"Ya, it's a thing." She said, "It's when you have random lapses of memory. You see, my brain is big, huge, but only so much information can fit inside of it at once. For example, I need to know the number of whips I must whip a pancake, how many clean socks everyone has, what to make for dinner. I could go on for days, but you get the picture."

"Hey, now, dads do that kind of stuff too. As you recall from our conversation a few seconds ago, we're not living in the prehistoric era."

"Your parents were pretty cool, I know. She brought home the bacon, and he fried it up in a pan. Very progressive."

"I mean, they really should have made a movie

about them." He said thoughtfully.

"They did. It's called Mr. Mom," She said, laughing.

"Oh, ya, I forgot about that. It's a shame that they never even got any royalties."

"I think that movie predates your birth by about a few years, so I am pretty sure that it is not about your parents, lovely though they were."

Sam smiled at the thought of them, and she did too.

So, what about a dad-brain? Can I claim that for forgetting your birthday?"

"I suppose. I mean, dad's brains are primarily known for the telling of terrible jokes and forgetting things like coffee creamer, and birthdays. "

"Oh, that reminds me,"

"Here it comes," she said, rolling her eyes.

"What do sprinters eat before a race?"

"What?" she sighed, knowing the punchline would be weird.

"Nothing, they fast!"

"Ugh!"

"Ok, one more," He said with his arms around her.

"No, you're going to make me go into labor because the baby wants to get away from these awful jokes."

"Please?" he said with a pout.

"Fine."

"When the grocery store clerk asked me if I want the milk in a bag, I always tell him, No, I'd rather drink it out of the carton!"

She laughed, then they kiss. "Now get to work," She said, "Mama needs a new pair of shoes."

"Funny."

"No, I am serious. I got a hole in my left one yesterday."

"You're such a dork." He said as he grabbed his keys.

"But I'm your dork." She called out after him. "And

if you value your life, don't forget the coffee creamer."

"Ya, ya, ya,"

"I mean it. I need my hazelnut creamer, or I am not going to survive another day."

He left, waving his hand behind him.

Sometimes she hated the fact that she didn't drive because it made it so very difficult to get around. For example, if she wanted to do something like pop to the store for coffee creamer, she would have to weigh out the fact that it could take as much as three hours to get there and back, against the things that she needed to get done that day. So, more often than not, she chose to stay home. Slowly as the years went by, she stayed home more and more, and before she knew it, being around other people began to cause her some anxiety.

She always dreamed of driving, and although her husband had given her several lessons, she kept asking herself, *what if somebody was coming towards me and she didn't make the right choice?* Sam's parents had died in a car accident, which only compounded her fear of driving. And after several years, she just put all thought of ever driving out of her head.

As a result, she had become more and more dependent on Sam to do things like shopping, taking the kids to the movies, sports, etc.

Because she spent so much time in her home, she was glad that she loved this house of theirs. It was like the house she had dreamed of living in as a child. It was a two-story Craftsman with hardwood floors throughout. The main floor held the usual array of kitchen, bathroom, living room, and dining room, with one bedroom located at the back of the house. Their hardworking and often sullen seventeen-year-old son Ethan inhabited that room.

On the top floor of the house were the remaining rooms. Natalie and Sam's bedroom was at the back of the house, twelve-year-old Cassidy's was at the front, eight-year-old Cloe's room was in the middle on the right, and

Cassidy's twin Connor's room to the left, next to another

bathroom. There was no attic to the house, so the only other

part of it was the basement. It was not Natalie's favorite

place to be as it was unfinished and a little dark and

spooky. But the washer and dryer were located there, so it

was a place that she spent a fair amount of time.

Sam loved the house as well, but it was a bit

bittersweet for him. He had lived in this house for most of

his life. And he was grateful to live in it now because on his

single salary one could not afford so grand a home. But if it

were up to him, he would not have chosen it to be this way.

As the only child, Sam inherited their house, which

had no mortgage. He only had to pay the upkeep and taxes

on it. Because of this, his salary was able to stretch further,

which allowed Natalie to fall easily into the role of staying

at home and taking care of the kids.

After the death of Sam's parents, both Sam and

Natalie slowly stopped seeing all their friends because they just wanted to be together. They knew that life was short, and they didn't want to miss out on being together for any part of it. By the time of their impending 18th anniversary, their home had become somewhat of an island for them, with occasional trips away from it for the sake of the children's activities. Because she kept to herself, she had to fight back anxiety anytime she ever took the kids to the park or walked to the corner store.

Natalie always felt a bit like an outsider in the neighborhood anyway. Like she didn't belong there. But she always felt so grateful to live in the house. It was her security blanket that she tried to keep always tightly tucked around her.

Sometimes though, she wondered what might have happened if she had gone to school to pursue a career in city planning. But even with all the washing, laundry, or cleaning up the living room for the million and first time that day, she was happy.

Sam's mom had encouraged her to go to school. She had put herself through school and landed her first gig as an architect before even starting to date. Natalie admired his mom. From what Sam said, she let nothing hold her back. She was great at her job. So, it was no surprise that she rose quickly through the ranks and ended up the head architect. And she was a great mom. She rarely missed one of Sam's games, always making sure to cheer extra loud for him. She always encouraged Sam to be the best he could be. Sam had been an only child. His parents had trouble conceiving a second. Natalie knew how blessed she had been to have her five.

Ethan, a straight-A student, had started attending Head Start, a program that allowed high school students to take college classes before they graduate. She was so proud of him, but also a bit jealous if she was honest.

She talked about signing up for some classes over

with Sam, who said, "Go."

At first, she misunderstood, "Fine. I'll leave. Sorry to bother you."

"I meant college." He said, "Go to college."

"What do you mean, go to college?"

"I don't know. I'll take a stab at it, though. Um, maybe go to college."

"That's crazy. I'm too old!"

"Says who?" Sam challenged her.

She stopped and thought for a moment and then she realized nobody did.

She imagined herself going to class and became filled with excitement. But, fear soon followed, with the thought of being stuck in a room full of people. *What if I say something stupid?* She wondered. Then when she factored in the time it would take to get there and back, as well as the kid's schedules, it seemed undoable, and she gave up the thought.

"I am way too busy, though. And the kids.." She argued.

"I will help. If it is important to you, then go. I've got your back."

She smiled at him. That is why she loved him so fiercely. He always had her back, no matter what. But fear crept in and took over. Soon she was telling herself *I will not mention it again. He will forget. And I will stay home where it is safe and warm and where everyone loves me.*

Natalie waddled her way over to the bathroom to relieve herself for what was the first of several times that day, as it is with most pregnant women. She caught a glimpse of herself in the mirror and smiled. Being pregnant always made her feel a bit like a superwoman. There was something about her body containing the tangible essence of the love that she and Sam had for one another, which made her feel invincible, though tired.

This pregnancy was a surprise. When Natalie didn't

get pregnant that first year after Cloe, she figured that her fertile years were behind her. She was wrong.

After she washed her hands and left the bathroom, she noticed Connor standing at her door, staring at her, expressionless. He usually did this when she was late coming down for breakfast.

"Good morning, honey," she said to Connor. "Are you ready for your pancakes?"

Connor nodded.

"Well, let's go then." She put her arm around him as they walked to the staircase.

When Connor was a baby, neither she nor Sam had any idea that he had autism. In fact, at that point, they had never even heard of the word before. They just thought he was extra quiet, that he was an introvert like her. Connor and Cassidy were so unlike in every way. She was outgoing; he was introverted. Cassidy played the flute in band class, Connor didn't take a music class as he was too sensitive to the loud music. She has a million friends, Connor, sadly didn't have any, unless you count the kids in his class at school.

When Connor started kindergarten, everything changed. He had such a hard time with everything required of him in kindergarten. Natalie dreaded the phone ringing back then, for it was usually the school calling her to come and take him home. Connor struggled through that whole year. So finally, the school had several specialists evaluate Connor. Then they had her come to a meeting to discuss their results

The had her take a seat on one side of a large conference table, while they all sat on the other side.

"Hello, I'm Brad Hurley. I oversee special education for the school district. I am overseeing the proceedings here today." He then introduced six other people. Then picked up a folder looked at its contents, then looked at her and said, "Your son has been evaluated by several of the people here. One of them, Mrs. Reynolds, could not make it today but has left the following report. It says that she has watched your son interact with his teacher and classmates on about three separate occasions. And has concluded that there is a strong possibility that Connor may have autism, though he will need to be further evaluated by your doctor."

Her mind raced. Autism? What is that? Is that contagious? Do I need to go to the doctor today? Will the other children get it?

"Mr. Sanders, will you please let us know what you observed." The meeting continued without her.

"Yes, thank you." Mr. Sanders said. "I…"

"Wait!" she interrupted, holding up her hand "Just wait!" She surprised herself by speaking up because she very rarely ever spoke up anywhere. But she couldn't keep silent. He had thrown a word out there that she had never heard before and claimed it was something that her son had as if he had a cold or the flu.

Lisa Cline

"What do you mean?" She asked. "What do you mean, she thinks he has autism? What is autism?"

From that point on, everything changed. It was clear now why things seem to be so hard for Connor. She had assumed that he acted as he did because she wasn't a good enough parent. She never seemed to be able to teach him how to do things like looking her in the eye. Now she realized that it was not about her but about who he was born to be. He was so many things, sweet, knowledgeable, thoughtful, funny, one of a kind. And she and Sam wouldn't have it any other way. They loved Connor and all their children immensely, never wanting them to be anything other than who they were born to be. And just like in life, when it came to breakfast, Connor was just a little bit different. The other kids mostly liked to eat cereal. Natalie was happy about this as it made her mornings easier.

Connor could not stand the smell of cereal and

insisted on pancakes for breakfast every morning. He loved pancakes so much that he researched them. Researching was something that he did when interested in a topic. And would usually share his results with her. She would often joke to Sam that she got more of an education from Connor than she ever did in school. He read somewhere that the precise number of whips one should whisk a pancake if they were to be perfectly fluffy, was between twenty to thirty whisks. From then on, he insisted upon watching as Natalie whisked the batter. He would be counting the number of whisks. She tried to get Connor to learn how to whisk the pancakes himself, but his issues with texture and certain smells stopped him. So, she whisked them as he stood back and watched.

When he counted to twenty, he would come and touch her hand. His doing this signified that she was too close and should put the whisk down. When she did, she saw the tension in his shoulders relax. He then sat at the table, and he waited while she cut it up into bite-sized pieces. Then pouring the syrup into a small bowl for him to dip the pieces into, she set it before him. He was like this with most things. He was very regimented, and everything always had to be just so.

Natalie started to clean up the mass from the pancakes just as Cassidy, Connor's twin sister, came in and grabbed the cereal from atop the refrigerator. Cloe followed right after her.

"Well, well. You're up early this morning, sweetie," she said to Cloe, whose bus to the elementary school came an hour after the twin's middle school one did.

"Sometimes I get up early," Cloe said with a shrug.

Natalie knew not to say good morning to Cassidy because Cassidy was not what one would call a morning person. Natalie once made the mistake of trying to have a conversation with her before 7 am. Cassidy just yelled at her, "Too early for words." And then she stormed off.

After getting the kids off to school, Natalie went back to bed. Natalie was not like those fit moms who spent their morning's jogging, and she wasn't one of those moms who had to have the house spotless every day either. Natalie was one of the moms that though she loved her kids, she also loved herself, taking time out when she needed it without feeling a tad bit guilty. Sam felt the same.

Natalie spent that day napping, cleaning, and texting Sam 3.25 million times things like, "Don't forget my creamer or you are sleeping on the couch." They always kidded each other. It was their way.

Usually, Sam was quick to respond. However, other than a quick text in the morning, Sam had not texted her back. She knew that sometimes he got busy at work, so she didn't think much of it. But when he was late getting home, she started to worry.

Later as she was dishing up food for the kids, she heard the door finally open. "You better not have forgotten my Hazelnut Coffee Creamer or no food for you." She said

in her best "Soup Nazi" voice.

She heard no reply, so she went into the living room

to investigate. Sam was leaning against the door, having

dropped his car keys and coat on the floor. He looked pale.

The last time she had seen him look so bad was at the news

of his parents' death.

Because he had no other close relatives, all she

could think was, he lost his job. She felt sick at the thought

but did not want to upset him. They always supported each

other, no matter what. "Don't worry. There will be other

jobs." She said, going to him.

"No, that's not it." He said without looking up. "I…

I'm sorry. I didn't get your coffee creamer."

"Oh, is that all? Man, you had me scared for a

second you big faker," She said, punching him playfully on

his arm.

Sam pulled a piece of paper out of his pocket and

31 Days to a More Peaceful You

held it out for Natalie. "I…I have cancer."

If you like this book and want to read more, please visit Amazon.com

To Know God as Father

(Non Fiction)

This Book is currently being revised and updated (As on 3/6/2020) It will soon have a New Title *Who Needs a Father Anyway*. It will have new updated chapters, including where needed, updated statistics.

Below is the first chapter from the **revised version**. It will be out by June 20th, 2020

Chapter One

She sat on the stoop waiting, her heart heavy and aching with anticipation so strongly that at times she wished she didn't have one. She had been there for an hour or more with no sign. Yet she wasn't too worried because she had her ace in the hole.

Lisa Cline

Another hour. She was lost in thought when her mama came up behind her and tried to gently guide her into the house. She would have none of it. Breaking from her mother's grasp, she said defiantly, "No! This time he is coming! He is. I know it deep, deep in me. He is!" Her words were firm, yet after her mother left her, she could not help but to let out a sigh and ask herself, "Is he really?"

As she sat there, she was tempted to give up many times. The next-door neighbor's family (a real one, she thought to herself) invited her to go bike riding with them. Her friends asked her to play a game of kick the can in the street. But she would not budge. She was convinced that this time he would come. Sure, in the past, he may not have always kept his word, but this time was different.

Today was her tenth birthday. Instead of the latest game, record, or book, she had asked for and (because money was tight) received only three things. They were a grown-up dress (not from the kid section), a pretty pink shawl, and a brand new pair of one-inch heels. She had never worn high heels before, so had practiced and practiced in them until she could walk without tottering. She couldn't wait to show off her new skill to her daddy.

He had once told her in the past that when she was more grown-up, he would spend more time with her. "Grown-up, how?" she had asked. He pointed to a woman who wore a long flowing dress with a pink shawl and high heels. From then on, she dreamed of the day when she would be old enough to wear high heels and a long flowing dress.

Another hour and the air was starting to get a chill in it. She could not tell, but her mother was inside frantically trying to get ahold of him to no avail. He was as he always was.

Another hour and the darkness started to descend. It was then she knew the truth.. you know, that thing that'll set you free. So she took off the high heels that she had practiced so hard to walk in, threw them away, and went inside. Heavy-hearted, she went straight to bed.

When her mother came in later to tell her how sorry she was, the little girl just shrugged her shoulders and remarked, "Who needs a father anyway?"

Although the story above was fictional, it represents many children in America today who long to be loved by their absent fathers.

Those of us who have grown up distanced from our fathers may sometimes feel alone in our fatherlessness. Yet statistics prove just the opposite. An estimated 24.7 million children (33%) live absent from their biological father[3]. Think about it! That's enough people to populate the whole of Australia plus Finland too. That's a lot of people! That must be why 72.2 % of the U.S. population says that the

---

[3] U.S. Census Bureau, Current Population Survey, "Living Arrangements of Children under 18 Years/1 and Marital Status of Parents by Age, Sex, Race, and Hispanic Origin/2 and Selected Characteristics of the Child for all Children 2010." Table C3. Internet Release Date, November 2010.

problem of absentee fathers is the most significant family or social problem facing America.[4]

And not only are fathers physically absent from their children, but many are (due to the death of someone close to them, a job, or just plain poor judgment) mentally absent as well. To have a father who lives in the same house but that is on a different planet is just as painful, if not more so. But remember the title of this book. Even when we have felt the most alone, God was there watching over us. We were never fatherless.

When our father is messed up, distanced, or quiet in our lives, we can be deeply wounded. If left unchecked, the wound can lead to anger, bitterness, and despair.

I know from experience that it is very easy to push feelings down instead of dealing with them. It seems as if we are solving our problem by doing so, but in reality, we

---

[4]National Center for Fathering, Fathering in America Poll, January 1999

are only prolonging the pain.

Imagine a garbage can that is stuffed full of dirty, smelly garbage. Not a pretty picture, is it? Now, I wonder how many of us would lift the lid and climb in for 50 bucks. I'm guessing probably not too many. Why? Because who wants to be sitting in smelly and (depending on how long it has been there) putrid garbage. But if that same garbage can was emptied out and given a good scrubbing and sprits of air freshener, the offer might be a little more tempting.

When we act out of our pain, we tend to make poor choices, which can result in things like loss of jobs, friends, dreams, etc. So, as a rule, when we find that we are spending most of our time alone, it is good to ask ourselves, "What would people see if they were to lift my lid?"

Statistics show that children of absentee fathers are more likely to do drugs, drop out of school, go to jail, etc.,

etc., etc. But what those statistics don't show, however, is the unlimited potential of those who get their garbage cans (minds) cleaned out of all the muck and mess and filled with the truth about who they are, whose they are, and who they were created to be. I am not talking about brainwashing here. I am talking about getting ahold of the word of God and finding out the truth about who we are.

…fix your attention on God. You'll be changed from the inside out. Readily recognize what he wants from you, and quickly respond to it. Unlike the culture around you, always dragging you down to its level of immaturity, God brings the best out of you, develops well-formed maturity in you.

(Romans 12:2 –The Message Bible)

Instead of holding bitterness, our minds can hold belief. Instead of clinging to anger, we can stick to the truth. And instead of being wrapped in sadness, we can be secure in the knowledge that we are loved and will never be forsaken. It is important to note, however, that until we learn to forgive our earthly father we will never be free. Why?

Because blaming fathers for being absent is a waste of time. No boy grows up and says, "I can't wait to have children so that I can ignore them." There was a reason that they chose - whether consciously or subconsciously - to distance themselves. That reason will always find its root in their own pain. What do I mean? I mean that maybe they were ignored by their fathers and so they learned to ignore it. Or maybe, they were abused growing up which caused them to subconsciously distance themselves from their children as a means of protecting them (kind of like an "I love you so much that I don't want to hurt you so I will keep my distance" sort of a thing).

Blaming fathers also prevents healing. Holding on to anger and bitterness will not change our past, but letting it go will change our future.

It does not take a psychiatrist to realize that we do damage to ourselves when we stuff down our feelings and hold on to our past hurts. I know how tempting it can be to want to hold on to anger. My father was absent from my life, about 99.9% of the time while I was growing up. It left me feeling worthless, and after years of trying everything that I could think of to fill the void, I was left broken-hearted and miserable. It wasn't until I let go of the anger and pain, and grabbed ahold of God that I was able to begin the healing process. Sometimes we may think that we have no choice about how we feel, but I am here to say that is a lie straight from the pit of Hell. We can choose to forgive. We can be free.

Blaming our fathers also keeps us from knowing God. It was not an easy leap to think of my father in Heaven in a different light than my Earthly father. I remember that I was about twenty-one when my mother tried to get me to read a book written by a grown child of an absentee father who found God as Father. I clearly remember thinking, "Forget that! I don't want a father. If God is a father, then that means He is not to be trusted." I told my mom I didn't want to read the book. And I didn't, though I now wished I had. Doing so would have saved me 15 years of pain.

The sad thing is that when I had that conversation with my mom, I was standing in a church library. Incredibly I went to church almost every Sunday, and yet I did not have the knowledge of what a wonderful Father God is. Why? Because I was stuck. My "right" to be angry and my distrust of any man that dare call himself father kept me stuck.

Little did I realize at the time that God is no natural man. Even the best father in the world cannot compare to God, nor should he try. Although God initially designed fathers to give us a small taste of Himself, it is essential to remember that just because some human man is messed up and dysfunctional, that doesn't mean that God is.

He is all you have ever wanted in a father and more! But He will never force a relationship with you. Though it is His desire to have an intimate relationship with each and every one of his children, He is not looking for "Furby-type" children. For those of you who don't know, a Furby is a toy that says many pre-programmed things, including "I love you." I remember thinking, how annoying would that be if my kids only said I love you because they were programmed to? Then I thought about free will, and why God gave it to us. I wrote a song titled "God Don't Want No Furby Kind Of Love." It was a terrible song, but its message was true. He wants us to come to Him because we realize that our lives are meaningless without Him.

If God was going to turn us into robots when we became Christians, then He would have made us robots, to begin with. So remember, although God first chose us, we have to choose Him.

God wants His kids (that's us by the way) to run to Him with arms and hearts wide open, ready to know, and love Him. But He realizes that some of us might take a while to get there. That's okay, though, because God is patient, and He lets us make our mistakes while He works quietly behind the scenes to draw us to Himself. Then as soon as we get close enough to grab on to Him, with even one pinky finger upturned, He will begin the slow and steady process of healing our hearts and setting us free from everything that keeps us from being who we were created to be, everything that keeps us from calling out to Him, "Abba Father."

In a few days, it will be Father's Day. It will mark the first time that my children have no Earthly father in whom to give their cards and funny presents too. Sadly, their father and my beloved husband of 18 years passed away just two months ago. It is hard being young, losing a parent, and wondering "why?" and "how come?" My heart aches for them, yet I can find peace in the fact that they are not alone. They still have not only a mother but also a Heavenly Father who deeply, deeply loves them. And you know what? He loves you too!

The truth is that, yes, our Earthly fathers are human. And yes, they can let us down. But how fortunate are we to have a Heavenly Father who will pick us up, dust us off, and set us on a path that He alone has laid out for us? A way that will lead us to the desires of our heart and will leave us with a peace that only our true father - our Heavenly Father - can give us?

To know God as Father means to know that He is a "Father to the fatherless" (Psalm 68:5), and He "will never leave you or forsake you" (Deuteronomy 31:6). So, get out that pinky, grab ahold, and watch as He heals your heart and takes you places you never even dreamed of.

On to your next sample…

31 Days to a More

Apologetic You (Devotional)

DAY 7 ~ How World Religions view God

One key and defining attribute of God that does not appear in any other

world religion or system is the biblical use of the term "Father."

Over 70 times in the New Testament alone, God is described

as "Father" to His children. No other major world religion describes

the relationship between its creator and its adherents in terms of a father.

– Ergun Caner

Knowing God as Father is the cry of every heart, so it is important to know how those of other faiths view him. What follows is a very basic summary of how 12 major world religions view God

- **Baha'i** ~ There is one god (no trinity) who is the same god that everyone in the world worships. No one can really know him on a personal level.

- **Buddhism** ~ There is no god; the god concept had its origins in fear. Belief in the potential of Humans "to develop into a Buddha - a perfected human being."[5]

- **Christianity** ~ One God, Three persons: Father, Son, and Holy Spirit.

- **Confucianism** ~One god who is distant. Their goal is to have a structured society.

- **Hinduism** ~ Differing beliefs about god. Belief in Monism/Polytheism/Monotheism. The cycle of rebirth is only broken through the individual's right living.

- **Islam** ~ There is one god (Allah) who is all-powerful and will allow into heaven those that are good

---

[5] Ven S. Dhammika. Buddhism and the God-idea. Found here:http://www.buddhanet.net/e-learning/qanda03.htm. Retrieved on July 14th, 2013

enough.

- **Jainism** ~ There are many non-creator deities. Belief that by being a non-violent person one will gain liberation from regeneration.

- **Judaism** ~ There is one God. The word father "When used of god … generally refers to the covenant relation between Him and Israel."[6]

- **Shinto** ~ There are many deities (some say as many as 8 million). One is the Sun Goddess Amaterasu. People are to serve the gods (called *kami*), but there is no afterlife.

- **Sikhism** ~ There is one god that the gurus teach about. The goal is to merge with god after over 8 million cycles of regeneration.

- **Taoism** ~ There are many deities. The goal is to be one with nature.

---

[6] "Father" Jewish Encyclopedia.com. Found Here "http://www.jewishencyclopedia.com. Retrieved on July 14th, 2013

- **Zoroastrianism** ~ There is one good god.

Salvation comes by being "good" (thoughts, word, and deed).

Ask yourself

How can I teach others that God is a loving father in a way they can understand?

31 Days to a More Joyful

You

Day 8 ~ Finding Joy

Find joy in everything you choose to do every job, relationship, home..it's your responsibility to love it or change it.

- Chuck Palahniuk

For most of us, the most significant part of our day is when we are working. And yet this is the area that we most often complain about, why? Because finding what we love to do and then doing it can be tough as well as scary. So, we stay working at a job we hate, preferring to stay stuck instead of stepping out.

Often, we do not step out because we are not quite sure what our talents are or what we should be doing with them. If that is you, it may be beneficial to ask yourself.

1. What is the one thing I do that when I do it,

everything in the world seems to fade away? What do I do that I lose hours doing? That is often the place where your passion lies.

2. What makes me excited to talk about? If you are a timid person and find yourself jumping into the conversation of strangers, chances are they are talking about something you love.

3. Who are the people (or what are the classes) that I have enjoyed learning from the most? So many times, people do not let their passion dictate their job. They get it stuck in their head that they should be (for example) a mathematician—when it was their cooking class that they most enjoyed.

4. What is my dream job? Sometimes the answer to this question is all it takes to find the job that brings you joy.

Ask Yourself

Lisa Cline

What am I doing to change the things in my life that are unproductive and bring me no joy? What steps am I willing to take today, this week, month and year, to get me to where I want to be next year?

APPENDIX 3 QUOTES

Day 1

God cannot give us a happiness and peace apart

from Himself,

because it is not there. There is no such thing.

C. S. Lewis.

Day 2

"Peace I leave with you; my peace I give to you.

Not as the world gives do I give to you.

Let not your hearts be troubled,

neither let them be afraid."

John 14:27, ESV

Day 3

You keep him in perfect peace

whose mind is stayed on you, because he trusts in

you."

Lisa Cline

Isaiah 26:3, ESV

Day 4

Do not be anxious about anything, but in everything by prayer and supplication with thanksgiving, let your requests be made known to God. And the peace of God, which surpasses all understanding, will guard your hearts and your minds in Christ Jesus.

Philippians 4:6–7, ESV

Day 5

The Christian needs to walk in peace, so no matter what happens, they will be able to bear witness to a watching world.

Henry Blackaby

Day 6

My people will abide in a peaceful habitation,

in secure dwellings, and in quiet resting places.

Isaiah 32:18, (ESV)

Day 7

We are not at peace with others because we are not

at peace with ourselves,

and we are not at peace with ourselves

because we are not at peace with God

Thomas Merton

Day 8

"Peace comes from being able to contribute the best

that we have, and all that we are, toward creating a world

that supports everyone. But it is also securing the space for

others to contribute the best that they have and all that they

are."

Hafsat Abiola

Day 9

Lisa Cline

If we have no peace, it is because we have

 forgotten that we belong to each other."

Mother Teresa

Day 10

A great many people are trying to make peace,

but that has already been done.

God has not left it for us to do;

 all we have to do is to enter into it.

Dwight L. Moody

Day 11

Peace Begins with a smile

Mother Teresa

Day 12

In peace I will lie down and sleep,

for you alone, Lord,

make me dwell in safety.

Psalm 4:8

Day 13

As we pour out our bitterness, God pours in his

peace.

F.B. Meyer

Day 14

The mind governed by the flesh is death,

but the mind governed by the Spirit is life and

peace.

Romans 8:6

Day 15

Therefore, since we have been justified by faith,

we have peace with God through our Lord Jesus

Lisa Cline

Christ.

Romans 5:1, ESV

Day 16

True peace consists in not separating

ourselves from the will of God.

Thomas Aquinas

Day 17

Being thankful can reap many benefits for you,

like peace and joy.

Jeff & Michelle Niederstadt

Day 18

Peace cannot be achieved through violence; it can

only

be attained through understanding.

Ralph Waldo Emerson

Day 19

Making peace with your own backstory,

 and accepting that not all of it is good, is vital.

Fearne Cotton

Day 20

The foundation of the Christian's peace is

everlasting; it is what no time, no change can destroy. It

will remain when the body dies; it will remain when the

mountains depart and the hills shall be removed, and when

the heavens shall be rolled together as a scroll. The

fountain of His comfort shall never be diminished, and the

stream shall never be dried.

His comfort and joy is a living spring in the soul,

a well of water springing up to everlasting life.

Jonathan Edwards

Day 21

Lisa Cline

God's peace comes when I choose to worship instead of worry.

Renee Swope

Day 22

You will find peace not by trying to escape your problems,

but by confronting them courageously.

You will find peace not in denial, but in victory.

 J. Donald Walters

Day 23

Peace is not the absence of conflict,

it is the ability to handle conflict by peaceful means.

Ronald Reagan

Day 24

Anything that costs you your peace is too

expensive.

Day 25

If you are depressed, you are living in the past

if you are anxious you are living in the future,

if you are at peace, you are living in the present.

Lao Tzu

Day 26

When a man's ways please the LORD,

He makes even his enemies to be at peace with him.

Proverb 16:7

Day 27

Peace is a daily, a weekly, a monthly process,

gradually changing opinions, slowly eroding old

barriers,

quietly building new structures.

Lisa Cline

John F. Kennedy

145

Day 28

Peace brings with it so many positive emotions

that it is worth aiming for in all circumstances.

Estella Eliot

Day 29

Blessed are the single-hearted, for they shall enjoy

much peace.. If you refuse to be hurried and pressed, if you

stay your soul on God, nothing can keep you from that

clearness of spirit which is life and peace. In that stillness

you know what His will is.

Amy Carmichael

Day 30

The day the power of love overrules the love of

power,

the world will know peace.

Mahatma Gandhi

Day 31

The LORD lift up his countenance upon you and give you peace.

Numbers 6:26

Lisa Cline

Please consider leaving a review

THIS WILL ONLY TAKE A MOMENT

Thanks for reading! If you enjoyed this book or got anything positive out of it, I would very much appreciate if you could take the time to review it on Amazon.

Not only will your review encourage others to read this book, it will also help me to keep writing new devotionals.

The link below goes right to the review for this book. And leaving a review only takes a moment of your time.

END NOTES

[i] Jonathon Lookadoo, "Peace," ed. Douglas Mangum et al., Lexham Theological Wordbook, Lexham Bible Reference Series (Bellingham, WA: Lexham Press, 2014).

[ii] Andrew Paterson, Opening Up John's Gospel, Opening Up Commentary (Leominster: Day One Publications, 2010), 126.

[iii] Lewis Foster, John: Unlocking the Scriptures for You, Standard Bible Studies (Cincinnati, OH: Standard, 1987), 156.

[iv] Earl D. Radmacher, Ronald Barclay Allen, and H. Wayne House, The Nelson Study Bible: New King James Version (Nashville: T. Nelson Publishers, 1997), Is 26:3.

[v] Warren W. Wiersbe, Be Comforted, "Be" Commentary Series (Wheaton, IL: Victor Books, 1996), 65.

[vi] Word in Life Study Bible, electronic ed. (Nashville, TN: Thomas Nelson, 1996), Is 32:16.

[vii] Wilhelm Gesenius and Samuel Prideaux Tregelles, Gesenius' Hebrew and Chaldee Lexicon to the Old Testament Scriptures (Bellingham, WA: Logos Bible Software, 2003), 550.

[viii] John D. W. Watts, Isaiah 34–66, Revised Edition., vol. 25, Word Biblical Commentary (Nashville, TN: Thomas Nelson, Inc, 2005), 829.

[ix] John D. W. Watts, Isaiah 34–66, Revised Edition., vol. 25, Word Biblical Commentary (Nashville, TN: Thomas Nelson, Inc, 2005), 829.

[x] Why You Need to Smile More" Neuronation https://www.neuronation.com/science/benefits-of-smiling

[xi] Roger Ellsworth, Opening up Psalms, Opening Up Commentary (Leominster: Day One Publications, 2006), 34.

[xii] Allen C. Myers, The Eerdmans Bible Dictionary (Grand Rapids, MI: Eerdmans, 1987), 161.

[xiii] William Arndt et al., A Greek-English Lexicon of the New

Testament and Other Early Christian Literature (Chicago: University of Chicago Press, 2000), 1066.

[xiv] Douglas J. Moo, Romans, The NIV Application Commentary (Grand Rapids, MI: Zondervan Publishing House, 2000), 250.

[xv] Douglas J. Moo, Romans, The NIV Application Commentary (Grand Rapids, MI: Zondervan Publishing House, 2000), 250.

[xvi] Michael P. Green, ed., Illustrations for Biblical Preaching: Over 1500 Sermon Illustrations Arranged by Topic and Indexed Exhaustively, Revised edition of: The expositor's illustration file. (Grand Rapids: Baker Book House, 1989).

[xvii] Garwood P. Anderson, "Righteousness," ed. Douglas Mangum et al., Lexham Theological Wordbook, Lexham Bible Reference Series (Bellingham, WA: Lexham Press, 2014).

[xviii] Johannes P. Louw and Eugene Albert Nida, Greek-English Lexicon of the New Testament: Based on Semantic Domains (New York: United Bible Societies, 1996), 556.'

[xix] Johannes P. Louw and Eugene Albert Nida, Greek-English Lexicon of the New Testament: Based on Semantic Domains (New York: United Bible Societies, 1996), 556.

[xx] "How Neuroscience Can Help Us Make Better Decisions" https://raywilliams.ca/neuroscience-can-help-us-make-better-decisions/

[xxi] Stephen Hopson. "7 Tips for Resolving Conflicts Quickly and Peacefully" Pickthebrain.com https://www.pickthebrain.com/blog/resolving-conflicts-quickly-and-peacefully/

[xxii] Robert J. Morgan, Nelson's Complete Book of Stories, Illustrations, and Quotes, electronic ed. (Nashville: Thomas Nelson Publishers, 2000), 295.

[xxiii] Andrew Knowles, The Bible Guide, 1st Augsburg books ed. (Minneapolis, MN: Augsburg, 2001), 83.

[xxiv] Warren W. Wiersbe, Be Counted, "Be" Commentary Series (Colorado Springs, CO: Chariot Victor Pub., 1999), 28.

[xxv] Lawrence O. Richards, The Teacher's Commentary (Wheaton, IL: Victor Books, 1987), 124